ury fielding all my life through, the new

e a child marie curie look into

nd everything bette arth

e nature of human beings not to be

've always thought my flowers had

of a collaboration between art and

d flowers in both hands japanese proverb the

ver wendell holmes there is material enough

of a score of cathedrals john ruskin bread

feed also the soul the koran if you truly

rywhere vincent van gogh nature, like a kind

our dreams and cherishes our fan-

iful places because they make them

dener can be made in one year, nor

arden is a solitary act michelle cliff in the

Barb,

May 2005

I couldn't resist

love, your big sis

P.S. Your garden looks amazing!!

Words

F⁰R GARDENERS T⁰ LIVE BY

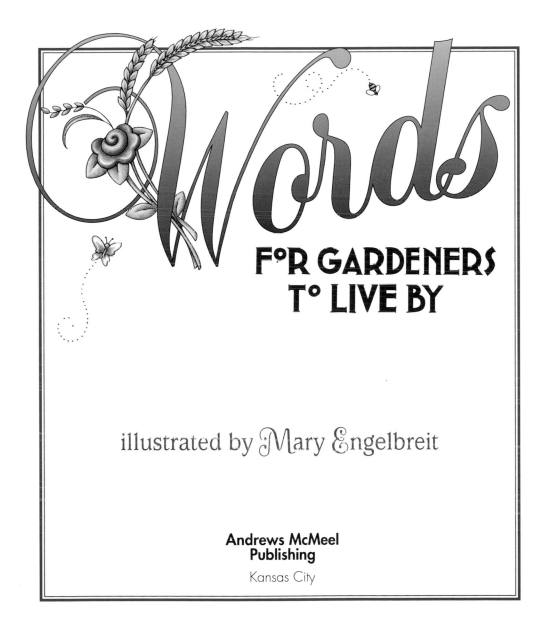

Words

FOR GARDENERS TO LIVE BY

illustrated by Mary Engelbreit

**Andrews McMeel
Publishing**

Kansas City

MARY ENGELBREIT™

www.maryengelbreit.com

ISBN: 0-7407-3518-7

Library of Congress Number: 20021118576

03 04 05 06 07 MND 10 9 8 7 6 5 4 3 2 1

Illustrations by Mary Engelbreit
Design by Delsie Chambon and Stephanie R. Farley

ATTENTION: SCHOOLS AND BUSINESSES
Andrews McMeel books are available at quantity discounts with bulk purchase
for educational, business, or sales promotional use. For information, please write
to: Special Sales Department, Andrews McMeel Publishing, 4520 Main Street,
Kansas City, Missouri 64111.

Contents

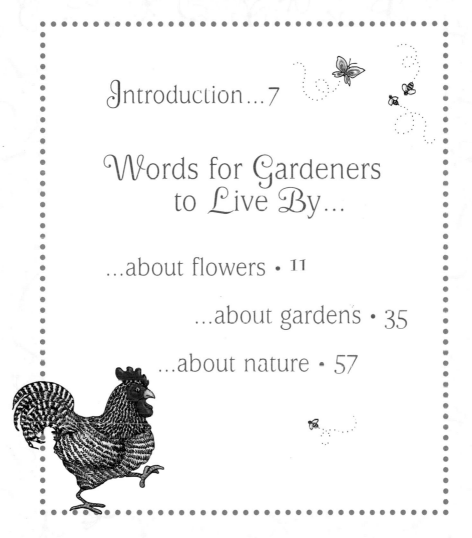

A few Words...
from
Mary Engelbreit

While sitting down to work on this book, I shuffled through a collection of my illustrations and was struck by the amazing array of flowers that seemed to bloom in every picture. A small cluster of sunflowers sits on a side table in one piece . . . a single daisy is tucked into a little girl's hatband in another . . . violets bloom profusely from a window box in the next. In fact, I was hard-pressed to find a picture that *didn't* include at least a small floral flourish.

My friends already know that (despite my best efforts) I do not possess the greenest thumb on my block. But I am a great appreciator of flowers—and of all things green and growing. In my life and in my work, flowers represent so many positive things to me: spirit, creativity, happiness, love, and most of all, the natural world's persistent inclination toward beauty. I agree wholeheartedly with the words of Alexander Pope,"All gardening is landscape painting." So, it's little wonder that flowers—and gardening—have played such an important role in my art.

Nature's artistry has always inspired visual artists, writers, and great thinkers.

From Georgia O'Keefe to Ralph Waldo Emerson, no one, it seems, was immune to the enduring charms of a simple flower. I guess it's no surprise that many of the writers whose words have inspired my art were inspired themselves by the fine and fragile gifts of the garden.

This book presents a collection of my artwork in which the wonder of nature, the glory of the garden, and of course, the beauty of flowers take a starring role. Presented along with the illustrations are some of my favorite writings on the same inspiring subjects. It is my gift to all those who lovingly tend a patch of earth in an effort to make this planet a more beautiful place.

Happy planting!

Mary

earth laughs in flowers *ralph waldo emerson*
i've always thought my flowers had souls *myrtle reed* happiness is to hold flowers in both hands *japanese proverb* bread feeds the body, indeed, but flowers feed also the soul *the koran* the amen! of nature... always a flower *oliver wendell holmes* f... may beckon towards us, b... speak toward heaven and G... *ward beecher* flowers are sunshine, food and medicine to the soul *luther burbank* there is material enough in a single flower for the ornament of a score of cathedrals *john ruskin* a single flower could impress

...about flowers

To create a little flower is a labor of ages.
—William Blake

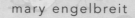

Flowers are
my music.

–Dr. Thomas Arnold

FLOWERS ARE SUNSHINE, food AND MEDICINE TO THE SOUL. ~LUTHER BURBANK.

𝒜 flower
touches everyone's
heart.
—Georgia O'Keefe

Flowers are love's truest language.

—Park Benjamin

13

Have you ever looked
into the heart of a flower? . . .
I love their delicacy, their disarming innocence,
and their defiance of life itself.
–Princess Grace of Monaco,
with Gwen Robyns

When you take a flower in your hand and really look at it,
it's your world for the moment.

—Georgia O'Keefe

flowers have
an expression
of countenance as much as
men or animals.
Some seem to smile,
some have a sad expression,
some are pensive
and diffident,
others again are plain,
honest and upright.
—Henry Ward Beecher

"How may I sing to thee and worship, O Sun?"
asks the little flower.
"By the simple silence of thy purity," answers the sun.

—Rabindranath Tagore

I am inclined
to think that
the flowers we
most love are
those we knew
when we were
very young,
when our senses
were most acute
to color and
to smell, and
our natures
most lyrical.
—Dorothy
Thompson

Flowers are works of art created by Nature for our pleasure.

— anonymous

I've always thought my flowers had souls.
— Myrtle Reed

BLOOM WHERE YOU'RE PLANTED

Happiness is to hold flowers in both hands.

—Japanese proverb

Bread feeds the body, indeed,
but flowers feed
also the soul.
—the Koran

Earth laughs in flowers.

–Ralph Waldo Emerson

Each flower is a soul opening out to nature.

—Gérard De Nerval

The Amen! of nature is always a flower.

–Oliver Wendell Holmes

Flowers may
beckon towards us,
but they speak
toward heaven
and God.

–Henry Ward Beecher

Flowers are nature's jewels, with whose wealth she decks her summer beauty.

–George Croly

A single flower could impress you with more gorgeousness than one hundred such.

–Yasunari Kawabata

God loved flowers
and created soil.
Man loved flowers
and created the vase.

—anonymous

People from a planet without flowers would think
we must be mad with joy the whole time
to have such things about us.

—Iris Murdoch

There is material enough in a single flower for the ornament of a score of cathedrals.

—John Ruskin

flowers...
are a proud assertion
that a ray of beauty
outvalues all the utilities
of the world.
—Ralph Waldo Emerson

Flowers have spoken to me
more than I can tell
in written words.
They are the hieroglyphics
of angels, loved by all men
for the beauty of the character,
though few can decipher
even fragments of their meaning.
—Lydia M. Child

BLOOM

© 19 ME 84

WHERE YOU'RE PLANTED

Deep in their roots, all flowers keep the light.

—Theodore Roethke

flowers are words
which even a babe may understand.

—Bishop Coxe

'Tis my faith that every flower

enjoys the air it breathes.

–William Wordsworth

To pick a flower is so much
more satisfying than just
observing it,
or photographing it . . .
so in later years,
I have grown in my garden
as many flowers as possible
for children to pick.

—Anne Scott-James

The first flower
that blossomed
on this earth
was an invitation
to an unborn song.
—Rabindranath Tagore

each garden has its own surprise

usan allen toth gardens are the result of a collaboration between art and nature penelope hobhouse in the spring, at the end of the day, you should smell like dirt margaret ... e a gardener, ... believe that what ... es down must come up lynwood ... all gardeners live in beautifu ... s because they make them so joseph joubert neither a garden nor a gardener can be made in one year, nor in one generation even "the gardener" to garden is a solitary act michelle cliff God almighty first plant ed a garden francis bacon true gardeners

...about gardens

A gard'ner's work is never at an end;
it begins with the year, and continues to the next.
-John Evelyn

IF YOU PRAY FOR RAIN,
BE PREPARED TO DEAL WITH
SOME MUD.

To own a bit of ground, to scratch it with a hoe,
to plant seeds and watch their renewal of life—
this is the commonest delight of the race,
the most satisfactory thing a man can do.

—Charles Dudley Warner

Let us not forget that
the cultivation of the earth
is the most
important labor of man.
When tillage begins,
other arts
will follow.
The farmers, therefore,
are the founders
of civilization.

–Daniel Webster

There are fairies at the bottom of our garden!

–Rose Fyleman

JUST LIVING IS NOT ENOUGH... ONE MUST HAVE SUNSHINE, FREEDOM, AND A LITTLE FLOWER.

I think this is what hooks one on gardening:
it is the closest one can come
to being present at the Creation.

—Phyllis Theroux

The garden...

was like a blossoming meadow,
from the house it suggested
a many-colored sea of petals
floating above the ground.
Over the surface of the sea
there were always butterflies
dancing, rather like flowers
detached from their stems.

—Janet Gillespie

To create a garden is to search for a better world.
In our effort to improve on nature,
we are guided by a vision of paradise.
Whether the result is a horticultural masterpiece
or only a modest vegetable patch,
it is based on the expectation of a glorious future.
This hope for the future is at the heart of all gardening.
—Marina Schinz

HAPPINESS MUST BE GROWN IN ONE'S OWN GARDEN

Gardens are the result
of a collaboration
between art and nature.
—Penelope Hobhouse

Working in the garden…
gives me a profound
feeling of inner peace.
Nothing here is in a hurry.
There is no rush
toward accomplishment,
no blowing of trumpets.
Here is the great mystery
of life and growth.
Everything is changing,
growing, aiming at something,
but silently, unboastfully,
taking its time.
—Ruth Stout

To garden is a solitary act.

—Michelle Cliff

*A*ll gardeners live in beautiful places
because they make them so.
–Joseph Joubert

SILENTLY,
ONE BY ONE
IN THE INFINITE
MEADOWS
OF
HEAVEN,
BLOSSOMED THE
LOVELY·STARS,
THE
FORGET·ME·NOTS
OF
ANGELS
—LONGFELLOW—

God almighty first planted a garden.
        —Francis Bacon

True gardeners
        cannot bear a glove
between the sure touch and the tender root.
        —May Sarton

Neither a garden nor a gardener can be made in one year,
        nor in one generation even.
                —"The Gardener"

When I go into my garden
with a spade and dig a bed,
I feel such an exhilaration and health,
that I discover that I have been
defrauding myself all this time
in letting others do for me
what I should have done
with my own hands.
But not only health but education
is in the work.
—Ralph Waldo
Emerson

There is a kind of immortality
in every garden.

—Gladys Taber

HOW DO YOUR CANDLES GLOW?

Each garden has its own surprise.

–Susan Allen Toth

The kiss of the sun for pardon,
         The song of the birds for mirth.
One is nearer God's heart in a garden
         Than anywhere else on earth.
                 –Dorothy Gurney

There's little risk in becoming
overly proud of one's garden
because gardening
by its very nature
is humbling.
It has a way of keeping
you on your knees.
—JoAnn R. Barwick

Like a gardener, I believe that
what goes down must come up.

—Lynwood L. Giacomini

The trouble with gardening . . .
is that it does not remain an avocation. It becomes an obsession.
—Phyllis McGinley

51

In the spring, at the end of the day,
you should smell like dirt.

—Margaret Atwood

Gardening is an exercise in optimism.
Sometimes, it is the triumph of hope over experience.

—Marina Schinz

This very act of planting
a seed in the earth
has in it to me
something beautiful.
I always
do it with a joy
that is largely
mixed with awe.
—Celia Thaxter

All gardening is landscape painting.

–Alexander Pope

Gardening has compensations out of all proportions
to its goals. It is creation in the pure sense.
—Phyllis McGinley

all nature wears one universal grin

henry fielding look deep, deep into nature and then you will understand every thing better albert einstein if you truly love nature, you will beauty every where vincent van go e, like a kind and smiling m ends herself to our dreams a cherishes our fancies victor hugo ly life through the new sights ature made me rejoice like a child marie curie it is the nature of human beings not to be able to leave nature alone margaret visse like a great poet, nature knows how to produce the greatest effects with

...about nature

The soil, in return for her service, keeps the tree tied to her;
the sky asks nothing and leaves it free.
– Rabindranath Tagore

If you truly love nature,
you will find
beauty everywhere.
–Vincent Van Gogh

Look deep, deep
into nature, and then
you will understand
everything better.
–Albert Einstein

NOBODY CAN BE IN GOOD HEALTH IF HE DOES NOT HAVE FRESH AIR, SUNSHINE, AND GOOD WATER.

— FLYING HAWK,
OGALA SIOUX CHIEF

FOR EVERY MAN THE WORLD IS AS FRESH AS IT WAS
AT THE FIRST DAY,
AND AS FULL OF UNTOLD NOVELTIES FOR HIM
WHO HAS THE EYES TO SEE THEM.
—THOMAS HENRY HUXLEY—

O the green
things growing,
the green things growing,
the faint sweet smell
of the green things
growing!

–Dinah Maria
Mulock Craik

All Nature wears one universal grin.

–Henry Fielding

Nature,
like a kind and
smiling mother,
lends herself to our dreams
and cherishes our fancies.
–Victor Hugo

All my life through,
the new sights of Nature made me rejoice like a child.
–Marie Curie

COME FORTH
INTO THE LIGHT
of THINGS,
LET NATURE
BE YOUR TEACHER
WILLIAM WORDSWORTH

A man is related to all human nature.

–Ralph Waldo Emerson

THE GOAL of LIFE IS LIVING in AGREEMENT with NATURE

MAKE A NEST of PLEASANT THOUGHTS.

I should only
observe with
regard to trees
that Nature has
been kinder to them
in point of variety
than even to its
living forms.
— Gilpin

Climb the mountains and get their good tidings.
Nature's peace will flow into you as sunshine
flows into trees.
The winds will blow their own freshness
into you, and the storms their energy,
while cares will drop off
like autumn leaves.
— John Muir

ALL OAKS *from* LITTLE·ACORNS GROW.

The creation of a thousand forests is in one acorn.
—*Ralph Waldo Emerson*

Nature is ever at work
building and pulling down,
creating and destroying, keeping
everything whirling and flowing,
allowing no rest but
in rhythmical motion,
chasing everything in endless song
out of one beautiful form
into another.

—John Muir

*It is the nature of human beings
not to be able to leave nature alone.*

–Margaret Visser

Like a great poet,
nature knows how
to produce the greatest
effects with
the most limited means.
—Heinrich Heine

In all things of nature
there is something of
the marvelous.
—Aristotle

Everybody needs
beauty as well as bread,
places to play in and
pray in, where nature may
heal and give strength
to body and soul.

—John Muir

Nature is whole and yet never finished.
–Goethe

Nature always tends to act in the simplest way.
–Bernouilli

Speak to
the earth,
and it shall
teach thee.

~ Job 12:8

Nature is the common, universal language, understood by all.
—Kathleen Raine

dream

Nature is painting for us, day after day, pictures
of infinite beauty if only we have the eyes to see them.
—John Ruskin

Nature does not hurry, yet everything is accomplished.

–Leo Tzu

It is not necessarily those lands
which are the most fertile
or most favored climate
that seem to me the happiest,
but those in which
a long stroke of adaptation
between man and his environment
has brought out the best qualities of both.

-T.S. Eliot

HAVE FAITH

Adopt the pace
of nature:
her secret
is patience.
–Ralph Waldo
Emerson

While the earth remaineth, seedtime and harvest,
and cold and heat, and summer and winter,
and day and night shall not cease.

–Genesis 8:22

A clear breeze has no price,
the bright moon no owner.

—Song Hun

True ecstasy hails neither from spirit nor from nature,
but from the union of these two.

-Martin Buber

Nature has been for me, for as long as I can remember,
a source of solace, inspiration, adventure, and delight,
a home, a teacher, a companion.

—Lorraine Anderson

Nature is often hidden, sometimes overcome,
seldom extinguished.

—Francis Bacon

Art is man's nature: Nature is God's art.

–Philip James Bailey

DRAW NEAR TO GOD AND HE WILL DRAW NEAR TO YOU.

JAMES 4:8

*N*ature gives to every time and season some beauties of its own.
—*C*harles Dickens

Look at the trees,
look at the birds,
look at the clouds,
look at the stars . . .
and if you have eyes
you will be able to see
that the whole existence
is joyful.

—Osho

I've always regarded Nature as the clothing of God.
—Alan Havhamess

*Nature uses only the longest threads
to weave her patterns so that each small piece of her fabric
reveals the organization of the entire tapestry.*
—Richard Feynman

How glorious a greeting the sun gives the mountains!
—John Muir

A sensitive plant
in a garden grew,
And the young
winds fed it
with a silver dew,
And it opened
its fan-like leaves
to the light,
And closed them
beneath
the kisses of night.
— Percy Bysshe Shelley

We do not see nature with our eyes,
but with our understandings and our hearts.
—William Hazlitt

EVER FORWARD, BUT SLOWLY.
VON BLÜCHER

The course of nature is the art of God.
—Edward Young

The best remedy for those who are afraid,
lonely or unhappy is to go outside,
somewhere where they can be quiet,
along with the heavens, nature and God.
Because only then does one feel
that all is as it should be
and that God wishes to see people happy,
amidst the simple beauty of nature.

—Anne Frank

Nature is our mother.

—Latin Proverb

Keep to moderation,
keep the end in view,
follow nature.

—Lucan

Let us permit nature to have her way.
She understands her business better than we do.
—Michel de Montaigne

Holy Mother Earth,
the trees and all nature
are witnesses of
your thoughts and deeds.
—North American
Indian saying

All that is sweet, delightful,
and amiable in this world,
in the serenity of the air,
the fineness of seasons,
the joy of light, the melody of sounds,
the beauty of colors, the fragrancy of smells,
the splendor of our precious stones,
is nothing else but Heaven
breaking through the veil of this world,
manifesting itself in such a degree
and darting forth in such variety
so much of its own nature.

—William Law

By viewing Nature, Nature's handmade art,
makes mighty things from small beginnings grow.
—John Dryden

all nature wears one universal grin

sights of nature made me rejoice li

nature, and then you will underst

laughs in flowers ralph waldo emerson it is th

able to leave nature alone margaret visser

souls myrtle reed gardens are the result

nature penelope hobhouse happiness is to ho

amen! of nature is always a flower

in a single flower for the ornament

feeds the body, indeed, but flowers

love nature, you will find beauty ev

and smiling mother, lends herself t

cies victor hugo all gardeners live in beau

so joseph joubert neither a garden nor a ga

in one generation even "the gardener" to